Misplaced

Erin Major

BookLeaf Publishing

Presentation by *BookLeaf Publishing*

Web: www.bookleafpub.com

E-mail: info@bookleafpub.com

ISBN: 978-93-95950-42-8

First edition 2022

ACKNOWLEDGEMENT

Thank you to those who read and relate to my poetry, for that we are connected.

To Feel is to Live

I am tired, I am lost
But at best I'm still going
Sometimes I wake up scared,
As though my insides are overflowing
Other times I wake up with my signature grin
Ready to seize the day
To know me is to know both of me,
Present and away
I am low but I am high
I am hiding but I am present
It is confusing, I can't deny
But to know me is to know both of me
And I am very much alive

Misplaced

I am lost
Amongst 1000 trees, I am lost

Surrounded by obscure dark paths, I am lost

No way out, no sign to be seen, no colour, the leaves are past their shades of green

It is dark. It's dark... but that does not mean it is cozy, oh to return to a place that feels homey.
With the fire on, cheeks go rosy
But instead, I'm stuck below sea

Chasing pockets of air, clothes on but my words strip me bare

This feels so unfair

But how dare I speak up
How dare I break down and erupt
You're right, there's bigger things going on, I'm sorry to interrupt.
Please carry on... I shouldn't have been so abrupt

How have I complained when I have all this luck, I have a place to stay, food to eat, so why do I still feel so... stuck

I am stuck

Surrounded by trails of possibility, I am stuck

Everything I see Is so beautiful but how do I make it mine, how will I stand out how will I fit in in a world that's already been designed

How can I be like them and leave something behind? All these questions float around in my mind

But no answers

Is it me?

Why does everyone seem so fine, what have they got that I don't?

Have they a map and a torch that shines?

To shine. I was supposed to shine. I was meant to be taught, prepared for the world. Grow my skin thick. But now I'm left with scars of the words you cut me with

To the bottom of my heart... they make me sick

Maybe, I am just sick. A faulty at birth, maybe I just don't work, I feel like my whole life has been a search, to find my way out of the dirt, to figure out why I keep getting so burnt. But I won't give up until I quench my thirst. To live. I want to live. To figure out what makes me tick

Yes, I am lost, but maybe just like keys, when they are found, they open us up to what we need

I will be found, I will follow my heart and listen to the beat of my own sound, I will forget what is meant to be and hear what IS me. It was there all along, fighting so hard to be loud, to remind me that as long as I'm alive... with a bit of time, it will be alright

It's okay if at times your feet lift off the ground

You will be found.

What We Were

Our love needed not time to grow

We just made sense
You were the sea
And I was the boat

I let you in
My heart made you space
We travelled each of our worlds
In a matter of days

We carved out our names
And left a piece of us
The second time we met
We walked back home,
Laughing at dusk

But those days
Could not lead to weeks

And I miss the way we felt

But I couldn't fight the wish
That you were somebody else

The last time I saw you
I looked into your eyes
And saw what we had

My stare promised you hope

My lies fell in your hands

The days that we had,
We danced with the world
Just us
The most powerful spell

Even though it's goodbye,
A little bit of you
Will stay frozen inside of me
Impossible to melt

Unrequited

my hands are empty
they long to give
to touch
to stroke
to pleasure.

your hands are strong
magnetic
they could save lives with the touch of a finger

but they do not desire to be in mine
how mine desire to fit in yours.

Clouds

I wish I was a cloud
Blowing in the wind
Or maybe a tree
One that stands tall and thin

I wish I was the sky
A home to all
I'd make everyone feel so big, that nothing felt small

I wished that I could wish for more
And make everything good, mine
But now I wonder why it was me I could never find

I wish to be me
Growing in my skin

Appreciating other beauty,
But still noticing mine within

Love yourself
And your life will begin.

Anything is Better than Nothing

I give too much of myself away
All this effort
In attempt to make you stay

So go on
Mould me how you like
Touch me like I’m made of
clay

Only worth feeling
If it's feeling you fuel my pain

I’ll be who you wish
I’ll be who you like

I’ll let you have my heart
And you can run for the knife

I’ll let you bruise my body
Just to feel your bite

I’ll even give you my neck
And let you suck my blood all night

If that is not enough
I suppose I’ll have to die
Maybe in another life
I’ll be worth your time

Warmth

The journey we are on at times makes us feel
lonely(in simple terms that is)
You may believe that everyone else is just 'so
fine' and all but you has a map,
or perhaps a torch that shines
But it's hard to believe one can feel so lonely in
a world crowded with other lost souls
Imagine we all just agreed we were a bit lost
It would make us feel a little less lonely
Or at least the warmth of another hand would
make us feel a little less cold.

Time's'ah'healer

Don't attempt to scrub off the skin you so desperately want to escape
It will only cause scars, cuts, and painful scabs
I once wanted the easy way out
I scrubbed and scrubbed and scrubbed and scrubbed
I was left with more pain than I had before
Yes, it is uncomfortable but only being present with your pain will lead to its healing
The more you try to escape and avoid, the tighter the skin, the lesser the breath

Slow down, get comfortable with being uncomfortable
It will shed when it's ready, from the inside out

Fly

There is no better feeling than the joy others feel
after beholding my art
Or my quirks being celebrated, the foibles that
set you and I apart
You see, when your foundations are built upon
being silenced
Anything you create has the potential to be torn
apart by your diffidence
So, any admiration sets my spirit alight, so
bright that it brings tears to my eyes.

To be creative, is to suffer. But how bittersweet
Almost like an unwanted but much needed
goodbye
Now, those farewells are tough, no doubt
But when one door closes, another one opens
So say goodbye to the distrust you hold against
yourself
And spread your origination
Someone might just notice your potential so
mute, that they are perplexed at how you held
your breath for so long, as if your limit is just
the ocean.

The Devil: Inside Us

The Devil resides in my heart
it's a good place to hide
Scream all you like, he's scared of no cry

Staring from my eyes
he feeds on my desire
Talking from my mouth
my truth sets on fire

No halo… Wings fall apart…
I can't outrun what I can't outsmart
I am not my own anymore, I have been rewired
I hear my distant screams, but my whispers are tired

He guides me to the verge, to make me a pledge
He said
"No more pain if you jump off the edge"

leaves lost

People come and people go, but what you learn from them will never leave you.

We are like trees, we have many branches. Each leaf that grows is a new beginning, a new lesson, a new journey, perhaps.

Those leaves will fall when the time is right. We get used to our leaves – they grow with us. But we also get used to our leaves lost, and new ones will grow.

Some stay longer than others, some fall too early, and some hang on for dear life.

We may feel empty, or cold, or even naked; but we need to make space for new leaves, new lessons.

Hold on to what they taught you. But let go when it's time. New leaves will blossom.

I Want to Feel Again

I have been defeated by my own ways

I thought that hiding my tears would solve all

But with no water, my flowers have become
decayed

I've re-wired who I'm meant to be

I'm reborn, I have been renamed

Let me feel the same as I think — I wish!

I can deal with it properly now — I insist!

"But you never dealt with it when we gave you
the pain, now you must only reminisce"

Give me another chance to feel it all, to accept
my hurt

My skin is empty, it needs emotion to quench its
thirst.

“Okay, I’ll send you pain. But you can’t look at it from your window anymore, you have to open the door”

Thank you! I will be waiting at the door!

“Remember though, it takes time to rekindle with your old friend. But don’t be afraid”

I will be afraid, I am afraid

But I need to finally look at it head-on, until my emotions return unveiled.

Give Yourself a Break

So as I looked around my room
finding something to do,
there wasn't much I could find so my curiosity grew.

I began to think about my past
and everything I am yet to find
The things I haven't done and the life I'm yet to design

What do I want and how do I get there? I thought
But how do I make it happen if I was never taught?

I got up off my bed and looked in the mirror
I saw what I had already accomplished,
and my thoughts became a little clearer

Look at the past self you lost but went onto save
-
Remember where you started and the progress you've made.

Komorebi

I once fell down a hole
A hole dug so deep that it felt impossible to
escape

I'd look up
the light felt so small
minuscule, even
it barely lit the tips of my fingers

And then it rained
The weight of the water consumed the hole
I was so cold I began to shiver
My neck turned so sore
I could barely hold it up to breathe

I was tired, but now even yawning was hard
I don't want to sink
But God
What do I do with this pain?

I looked up at the tiny piece of light once more
wishing it would grow as big as the sun
And then I heard it speak

"Stop wishing I was big and powerful!
Let me be as I am! You'll see!"

It was so mad that it left.

It was even darker than before
All I wanted was that tiny bit of light back
I wished for it so hard that I forgot the sun once before existed

I screamed, cried, and almost choked
"You were perfect as you were! I'm sorry! Please return!
You were the only thing that kept me going!"
I lost balance, I couldn't see anything and the water was even colder.

The light shyly peaked back
I was so grateful for its return
I jumped and splashed and found such joy in twinkling my fingertips in the dim light
Why didn't I do this before!?

There's always a way to find light -
even in the darkest of times.
Small is better than none

Maybe it'll even grow.

make sure your friends are okay

Half full, seemed his cup
so vibrant
so bright
He'd walk into a room
and light it up

But little did they know

The darkness was not missing

Just hidden

Home to his heart.

"Clumsy"

I noticed it the day I met her. How she stood in the world.
She was never steady on her feet. She was ready to stop anyone but herself from
falling... As if it was her who didn't belong, and it was only a matter of time before
the world questioned her presence, too. She realised that if she was of use to
others, rejection was unlikely and she could get on.
But if she were to fall, would they run to catch her?
She never cared.
As it was easier to trip up and be stepped over than to be tripped up, and get stepped on.

Nostalgia

The wind whistles not with woe
But with ease
Like its reading us a bedtime story
It's breath kisses my forehead
And plays ever so slightly
With my baby hairs
I fall asleep,
Peacefully

Martha

Hold onto them tight dear -
tight so they know they are never alone,
but not so tight that they never feel lonely.

Everyone needs to feel lonely at least once.
Too much suffocation and they will never feel
the need to make decisions for themselves -
but too little guidance and they wont have the
tools to make the most out of their lives.

Our First Time

He pranced around and skipped over my cracks
like that game we played as kids

My scars on show
his hands placed over them, gently
as if it all still stings

A trance connecting our eyes
he captured every bit of my face
as if he couldn't again for many years

We banished the experience of normal
as though there were no antonyms for weird

I said lets let go of all our fears –
Lets pretend it's as simple as autumn leaves
blowing away in the wind

Lets make our love for life so loud it sounds
beautiful
like a church echoing its hymns

Midnight Reflection

It was intense, and warm, and kind
It was just as much enlightening and cathartic
too

But I don't feel fear when I imagine life without
you
So if this isn't love, then what is this?

I know that I love how you introduced me to the things I can't live without, I love that we changed each other for the better, I love that it was you who led me to the person I am today, and I love that this means you are stained all over me forever

But most importantly,
I love that you made me love more of me

For that, I will always live a happier life than
before
With or without you

Perhaps love is a thing that exists inside of us
Maybe it's constantly searching for another
being with suitable lessons, and when found, it

hops into their body, drawing us to them. Maybe it hops and hops until we've learnt enough and when we know what we truly want and deserve, it'll hop one last time

You were not the one, but you led me to the one I needed the most

And for now, that is me.

we are all just winging it

Sometimes
I cant believe I'm a human that does human things
Because at times life can feel like a thick piece of string
And I'll always just be the blunt needle with its eye too thin
Sometimes I forget where I'm going
Or I sprain my ankle once in a while
But If life is about driving with direction
Then I'l probably always be the old Satnav that's lost all its connection

I'd rather explore anyway

www.ingramcontent.com/pod-product-compliance
Lightning Source LLC
Chambersburg PA
CBHW051754130826
49812CB00033B/1152
9789395950428